Spiny Lobsters

by Lindsay Shaffer

READERS

BELLWETHER MEDIA • MINNEAPOLIS, MN

Note to Librarians, Teachers, and Parents:

Blastoff! Readers are carefully developed by literacy experts and combine standards-based content with developmentally appropriate text.

Level 1 provides the most support through repetition of high-frequency words, light text, predictable sentence patterns, and strong visual support.

Level 2 offers early readers a bit more challenge through varied simple sentences, increased text load, and less repetition of high-frequency words.

Level 3 advances early-fluent readers toward fluency through increased text and concept load, less reliance on visuals, longer sentences, and more literary language.

Level 4 builds reading stamina by providing more text per page, increased use of punctuation, greater variation in sentence patterns, and increasingly challenging vocabulary.

Level 5 encourages children to move from "learning to read" to "reading to learn" by providing even more text, varied writing styles, and less familiar topics.

Whichever book is right for your reader, Blastoff! Readers are the perfect books to build confidence and encourage a love of reading that will last a lifetime!

This edition first published in 2020 by Bellwether Media, Inc.

No part of this publication may be reproduced in whole or in part without written permission of the publisher. For information regarding permission, write to Bellwether Media, Inc., Attention: Permissions Department, 6012 Blue Circle Drive, Minnetonka, MN 55343.

Library of Congress Cataloging-in-Publication Data

Names: Shaffer, Lindsay, author.
Title: Spiny Lobsters / by Lindsay Shaffer.
Description: Minneapolis, MN : Bellwether Media, Inc., 2020. | Series: Animals of the coral reef |
  Includes bibliographical references and index. | Audience: Ages 5-8 | Audience: Grades K-1 |
  Summary: "Relevant images match informative text in this introduction to spiny lobsters. Intended for students
  in kindergarten through third grade"-- Provided by publisher.
Identifiers: LCCN 2019033040 (print) | LCCN 2019033041 (ebook) |
  ISBN 9781644871355 (library binding) | ISBN 9781618918178 (ebook)
Subjects: LCSH: Spiny lobsters--Juvenile literature.
Classification: LCC QL444.M33 S498 2020 (print) | LCC QL444.M33 (ebook) | DDC 595.3/84--dc23
LC record available at https://lccn.loc.gov/2019033040
LC ebook record available at https://lccn.loc.gov/2019033041

Editor: Betsy Rothburn   Designer: Laura Sowers

Printed in the United States of America, North Mankato, MN.

Table of
Contents

Life in the Coral Reef

Caribbean spiny lobster

Spiny lobsters are **crustaceans**. They live in warm waters around the world.

They live well in the coral reef **biome**!

Caribbean Spiny Lobster Range

N
W E
S

range = ☐

Many **predators** live in coral reefs. Spiny lobsters have **adapted** to stay safe.

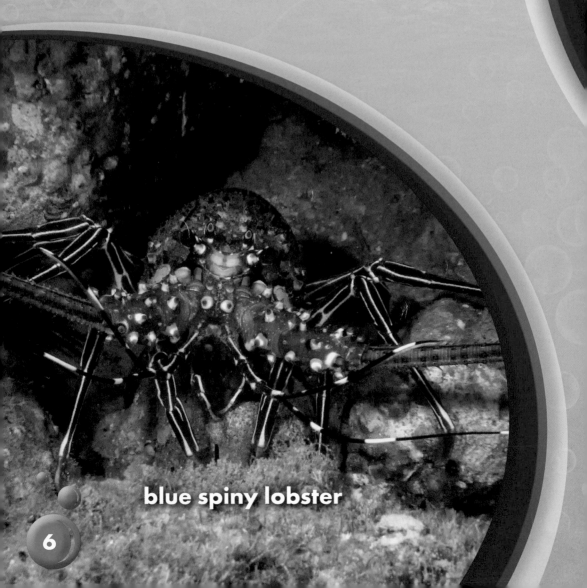

blue spiny lobster

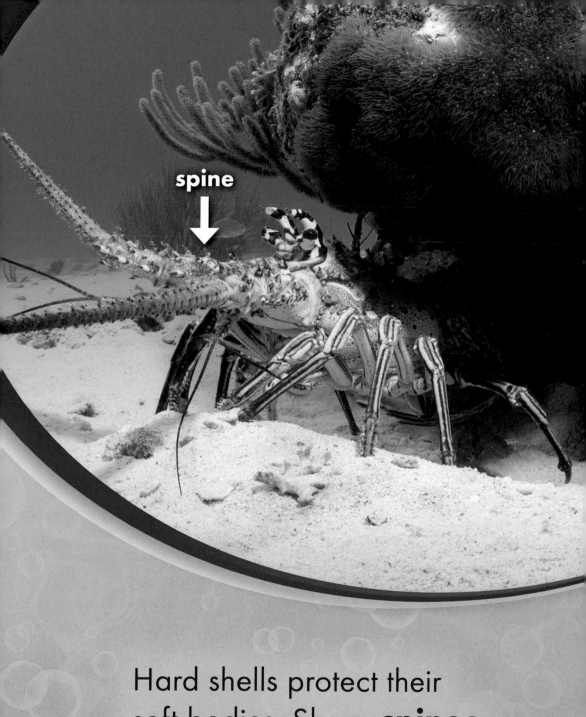

spine

Hard shells protect their soft bodies. Sharp **spines** poke predators!

Strong tails help the lobsters swim backwards. They speed through busy coral reefs.

Special Adaptations

sharp spines

hard shell

strong tail

long antennae

They swim into cracks to hide!

Safe and Warm

Octopuses and sharks try to eat spiny lobsters. But the lobsters scare them away.

They rub their **antennae** against their heads. This makes a loud buzzing sound!

antennae

The lobsters can escape bites. They drop their legs or antennae to break free.

The parts quickly grow back!

Winter brings cool water to coral reefs. Spiny lobsters must **migrate** to warmer places.

They travel in groups to their new homes!

Caribbean Spiny Lobster Stats

Least Concern	Near Threatened	Vulnerable	Endangered	Critically Endangered	Extinct in the Wild	Extinct

conservation status: least concern

life span: up to 20 years

Caribbean spiny lobsters migrating

Looking for Food

Spiny lobsters are **omnivores**.

They look for foods like fish and **algae**. They will even eat other lobsters!

Spiny lobsters look for food at night. They sniff out tasty meals.

Spiny Lobster Diet

red cushion
sea stars

kelp

purple sea urchins

They use their front legs
to scoop up **prey**.

Strong jaws help the lobsters open clamshells.

Spiny lobsters are
well adapted to the
coral reef biome!

Glossary

adapted—changed over a long period of time

algae—plants and plantlike living things; most kinds of algae grow in water.

antennae—feelers on a spiny lobster's head that help it touch, smell, and taste

biome—a large area with certain plants, animals, and weather

crustaceans—animals that have several pairs of legs and hard outer shells

migrate—to travel from one place to another, often with the seasons

omnivores—animals that eat both plants and animals

predators—animals that hunt other animals for food

prey—animals that are hunted by other animals for food

spines—sharp points that stick out from a spiny lobster's body

To Learn More

AT THE LIBRARY

Adamson, Heather. *Lobsters*. Minneapolis, Minn.: Bellwether Media, 2018.

Hulick, Kathryn. *Coral Reefs*. New York, N.Y.: AV2 by Weigl, 2019.

Siemens, Jared. *I Am a Lobster*. New York, N.Y.: AV2 by Weigl, 2018.

ON THE WEB

FACTSURFER

Factsurfer.com gives you a safe, fun way to find more information.

1. Go to www.factsurfer.com.

2. Enter "spiny lobsters" into the search box and click 🔍.

3. Select your book cover to see a list of related web sites.

Index